CO-AUU-944

UNIVERSITY OF
ILLINOIS LIBRARY
AT URBANA-CHAMPAIGN
MUSIC

780.72
F92
no. 3

music

from research
to the music classroom no. 3

Teaching
Instrumental
Music

UNIVERSITY OF ILLINOIS
LIBRARY

By George L. Duerksen

MENC

The Library of the

MAY 12 1976

University of Illinois
at Urbana-Champaign

The person charging this material is responsible for its return to the library from which it was withdrawn on or before the **Latest Date** stamped below.

Theft, mutilation, and underlining of books are reasons for disciplinary action and may result in dismissal from the University.

To renew call Telephone Center, 333-8400

UNIVERSITY OF ILLINOIS LIBRARY AT URBANA-CHAMPAIGN

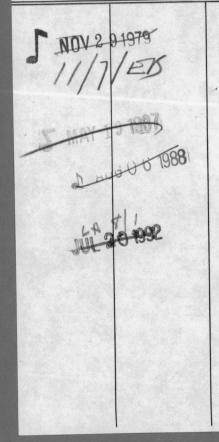

NOV 2 9 1979

11/7/ERS

MAY 19 1987

AUG 0 6 1988

JUL 20 1992

L161—O-1096

from research
to the music classroom no. 3

Teaching
Instrumental
Music

By George L. Duerksen

Copyright © 1972 by
Music Educators National Conference

Printed in the U.S.A. All rights reserved. No part of this publication may be reproduced or transmitted in any form or by any means, electronic or mechanical, including photocopy, recording, or any information storage and retrieval system, without permission in writing from the publisher.

Library of Congress Catalog Card Number 72-075045

Music Educators National Conference
1201 Sixteenth Street N.W., Washington, D.C.

CONTENTS

FOREWORD

Research findings can be of much value in the teaching of music if they are considered cautiously and realistically. The results of any study are true for the particular circumstances in which the study was conducted, and they may or may not apply to different situations. Also, a host of factors influence the results of research involving human beings. Such diverse matters as the method of teaching; the length of time the experiment was conducted; the number, age, and abilities of the persons studied; the extent of the controls maintained; and even the knowledge by the subjects that they were involved in an experiment may significantly affect the outcome. For these reasons, a single study should not be considered final or conclusive. Research provides information, not proof in the usual sense of the word. Clearly, the more studies conducted in an area, the more information there is available, which, if reasonably consistent, encourages one to place greater confidence in the findings.

Research data must be interpreted, and all interpretation is subjective. For example, the ability of a group of twelve-year-olds to recognize intervals aurally may have been improved somewhat under certain conditions by a certain teaching method. Although the results achieved are not open to question (provided the research was carried out in a competent manner), the importance and meaning of the findings to the teaching of general music classes are a matter of judgment. Therefore, the interpretations of the research data presented in this publication are those of the author, and they do not necessarily represent the opinions of the Music Education Research Council of the Music Educators National Conference.

Research, even with all of its frailties, is the best way mankind has yet devised for unearthing objective truth. Intuition and personal opinion have their place in life, but they do not provide objective information. Because objective data can help one to make more intelligent judgments, research has a valuable place in music education. Thus, the publication of the series *From Research to the Music Classroom.*

TEACHING INSTRUMENTAL MUSIC

In helping develop and modify a student's musical behavior, music education assumes the role of a behavioral science. The music educator needs full understanding of the interaction of genetic, psychological, cultural, and other environmental factors in the development of human musical behavior if he is to help his students develop to the best of their potential. Where can the music teacher get information about these factors? Competent research provides some information, but final answers are never assured. Each application of a principle requires evaluation of its appropriateness and effect.

Although gaps in knowledge remain and the validity of some studies may be questioned, the increasing quantity of research in music education and related disciplines provides a growing source of help for the instrumental music teacher. Individuals tend to accept research results that agree with their own opinions, and to discount those that do not. Studies reported in this monograph sometimes have implications that disagree with things music educators have "known" for years. Such implications deserve consideration, even though teachers believe them to be incorrect. The history of man contains many examples of research findings that were initially rejected because they disproved what was "known." Data, of course, are subject to interpretation, and this report is an interpretation of what research suggests for teaching instrumental music.

The Instrumental Program

Predicting Success for Individual Students

A variety of devices is used to estimate a student's potential for success in instrumental music. These devices include standardized music tests called by a variety of names, including musicality, aptitude, talent, musical intelligence, achievement, appreciation, and sensitivity tests, as well as tests published by instrument manufacturers, intelligence tests, academic grades, and evaluations of physique. Such evaluations are sometimes used to encourage or discourage a child from participating in instrumental music. How accurately do they predict success?

Studies at different levels ranging from kindergarten through college lead to a single conclusion: scores on presently available standardized tests, used alone or in combination, do not correlate well with success or failure in instrumental music and cannot be used as the only predictor of whether or not an individual will succeed. Success in instrumental music has been measured in several ways in these studies, but however measured, correlations with standardized test scores seldom reach 0.50. While this degree of correlation is of value in research and in making predictions for groups, it is not high enough to warrant confidence in predictions for individuals. High scores on the various tests do not assure that the student will succeed, nor do low scores assure that he will not. The data suggest that it is not justifiable to bar students from instrumental music programs solely on the basis of their scores on the aptitude type of test.

In several studies predictions were based on a battery of tests, but the best single test often proves nearly as good a predictor as the entire battery. A recent study investigated the predictive power of the *Gordon Music Aptitude Profile*, the *Lorge-Thorndike Intelligence Test*, the *Iowa Tests of Basic Skills*, and a set of specially constructed music achievement tests for a group of beginning instrumentalists in elementary school. Each test made some contribution in the predictive battery. Although the students who remained in the instrumental program had higher average scores on the Gordon tests than those who dropped out, neither the Gordon tests nor the combined battery could predict who would drop out and who would remain (79). Another study evaluated the pitch section of the *Seashore Measures of Musical Talents*, the *Terman Intelligence Test*, and an estimate of musical achievement. Intelligence was a better predictor than the other measures, but no measure correlated well enough for accurate predictions of individual success (60).

Research at the secondary school and college level shows prior achievement to be the best predictor of success in music. For instance, one study (which included the *Gaston Test of Musical-*

6

ity and the pitch and tonal memory sections of the *Seashore Measures of Musical Talents*) found the best predictors for college achievement of music education students to be high school achievement (as indicated by grades) and achievement tests in music theory and ear training (26). Another study found that academic achievement and intelligence test scores were about equal in predicting success for beginning band students. Even for these predictors, however, the correlations with success were too low (correlation of .50 for intelligence and success, .49 for academic achievement and success) to be of predictive value for individuals (50).

Although standardized test scores do not provide information that facilitates accurate prediction of success, they can help the teacher anticipate particular areas that may be troublesome for his students. In one study, beginning instrumental students took the *Gordon Music Aptitude Profile*. Their teachers used the test results in planning instruction. These students made appreciably greater progress than those whose teachers did not have access to test scores. Instruction based on test profile data proved particularly beneficial for those in the highest and lowest ability groups (25).

Choosing an Instrument

How can a student choose an instrument on which he is likely to succeed? Establishing criteria for choice presents a perplexing problem. Physical measurements such as dental formation, lip thickness, and finger taper have not been successful in predicting success on specific musical instruments (40). A comparison of college instrumental majors and nonmusic majors on ten different psychomoter ability tests revealed no significant differences between the groups (48). Among 914 students questioned in one study, the most popular reason for choosing an instrument was "I liked the way it sounded." The next most popular reasons, in descending order, were "the instrument just intrigued me," "it looked easy to play," "my father and/or mother thought it best for me to play," "it was needed in the band," and "we had the instrument at home." Most students cited several reasons, rather than just one (75). The most popular reason cited, the appeal of the instrument's sound, seems particularly interesting in light of results of a different study. Compositions written originally for orchestra, for band, and for other media were recorded by both

band and orchestra. Students listening to the recordings con-
sistently chose the orchestra performances over the band performances (66).

Appropriate Grade Level to Start Learning an Instrument

The question of the best grade at which to begin instrumental
instruction becomes increasingly important as the curriculum
expands and school budgets become tighter. School instrumental
instruction traditionally begins in intermediate grades, although
the Suzuki method of teaching has demonstrated that violin
instruction can begin earlier. Piano students often begin private
lessons during the primary grades. To date the research studies
provide only tentative direction. One investigation in the 1940s
found there was little advantage to beginning work on a wind
instrument before about the eighth grade, the age of 13 (52). A
more recent study indicates that the seventh grade seems to be an
optimum level for starting instrumental instruction, and that
playing experience preliminary to this is not necessary for
development of successful performance skills (19). Additional
careful research is needed to increase confidence in these
suggested optimal levels.

Is it wise to take a student out of another class for
instrumental instruction? Students typically are dismissed from
the classroom, where academic work is continued, in order to
take part in instrumental classes. Not much research has been
done in this area, but a recent study shows no difference in
average scores on the *Iowa Tests of Basic Skills* between students
who had missed class for instrumental study and those who had
not (29).

Preinstrumental Experience

Several reasons are advanced for using preinstrumental instruments in the elementary school music program. Some believe
such experience leads to greater success in later instrumental
performance. Work on such instruments also may lead to
development of other musical competencies. Research indicates
that junior high students can succeed in instrumental performance without prior work on preinstrumental instruments (45).
However, fourth-grade students performed better at the end of an
eighteen-week session that included four weeks study using
drumsticks, three weeks using flutophones, and eleven weeks in a
heterogeneous instrument class than did others who studied all

8

eighteen weeks in a heterogeneous instrument class (71). A different study found that fourth-grade students whose music class played preinstrumental melody instruments scored significantly higher on tests of musical aptitude and verbal musical achievement than those whose class did not play such instruments (2). These findings indicate that preinstrumental instrument experience, though not essential for success in later instrumental performance, may help raise the student's general level of musicianship and knowledge. The findings indicate that time in the upper elementary grades might be spent better in general music study, including the learning of preinstrumental instruments, than in working on traditional band and orchestral instruments.

Readiness for Instrumental Instruction

In order to learn to play a musical instrument successfully, a student must make several discriminations. He must be able to distinguish sounds and to distinguish visual patterns of musical notation. The term "readiness" sometimes is used to indicate that a child is developmentally sufficiently advanced to be able to learn specified discriminations. Research gives some information about important discriminations.

A study of the perception of instrumental tone color by children of nursery school age revealed marked differences in ability to discriminate between pairs of instrumental tone qualities. Over 50 percent of the children fifty-four through sixty-three months of age were able to differentiate between the tones of the trombone and the French horn, violin and trumpet, flute and violin, cello and bassoon, and oboe and muted trumpet. Wide differences existed between students at every age tested (1). Another study revealed that music educators perceive nuances in tone quality that many high school students do not. Instrumental music students at successively higher class levels exhibited only small increases in skill in discriminating tonal nuances (4). This study indicates that mere participation in instrumental music during high school is not very effective in developing skill in discriminating nuances in tone quality. If the instrumental teacher intends for his students to develop discriminative listening skill, he should, therefore, teach specifically for this outcome.

Music teachers often consider awareness of differences in pitch, duration, and quality to be involved in readiness to read musical notation. A study of the perception of musical sounds by

9

students in grades one through six provides some information about the listening skills of children at the time they typically begin work in instrumental music. Although listening skill and grade level were found to be related, only small differences in listening skill appeared between adjacent grade levels. Within each grade level children differ markedly in musical competence and aural skill (53). Further research leads to the belief that some of the notation found in elementary school music books is more difficult than the typical elementary school child can readily perceive (54). Notation of similar difficulty is likely to occur in instrumental music.

Levels of reading difficulty estimated by experts may not coincide with levels of difficulty experienced by students. In one study, instrumental music students attempted to sight-read exercises arranged in a supposedly logical sequence of difficulty. In many cases students were able to play exercises that were expected to be difficult, but had trouble with those that were expected to be comparatively easy. The study indicates that students may read different pitch and rhythm patterns more readily because of individual differences in students rather than because of a logically determined sequence of complexity (43).

The reported studies about perception, discrimination, and sight-playing of musical notation emphasize the need for individualized instruction in instrumental music. Students at each grade level from elementary school through high school exhibit a wide variety of skill in auditory and visual perception.

In one sense, musical listening skill may lead a beginning instrumentalist to problems in the development of correct physical motion and posture while playing. Students with musically-trained hearing made significantly more errors in physical position and movement while learning to play violin than did those without such training. Students with untrained hearing were better at playing tones in tune with proper physical form; those with trained hearing played tones in tune, but often with improper hand position (35). At early stages of instrumental performance, it is possible to play simple tunes without fine physical position. Correct playing position becomes progressively important as the music becomes technically more difficult.

Class and Private Instruction

No matter what the grade level, questions of class organization confront the instrumental music teacher. Which is best, class or private instruction? Several investigations compare the effectiveness of class and private instruction. A study of piano instruction in elementary school levels revealed no large differences between the achievement of students taught in classes and those taught privately, although a few small differences were evident. Students taught in class were slightly superior to those taught privately in knowledge of musical rudiments, skill in sight reading, and recognition of compositions. Private students were slightly superior to class students in prepared performances (34). A comparison of the performance skill developed by beginning voice students in secondary schools showed that those taught in class sang as well as those taught privately (68). In one study, students taught privately tended to perform better than those taught in class (72), but another study, with more controls, found no significant difference in performance skill between students who had studied privately and those who had studied in heterogeneous classes (67).

Thus it seems that beginning students can learn to perform either in homogeneous class or through private instruction. Is there any advantage in grouping instrument classes homogeneously or heterogeneously? When fourth, fifth, and sixth grade beginners in homogeneous and heterogeneous instrumental classes were compared, no significant differences were evident between classes, either in attitude toward music or in performing skill (61). Unfortunately, to date very little study has been conducted on this important question.

Instructional Methods

Motivation, Reward, and Reinforcement

Research in the psychology of instruction provides information useful in making decisions about instructional approaches and techniques. In this category are studies of motivation, reward, reinforcement, punishment, the biopsychology of learning and remembering, and the various techniques for efficient learning of music.

Evidence from the psychology of instruction indicates that reward or reinforcement should be a useful source of motivation in teaching music. Rewards are often labeled intrinsic or extrinsic. Intrinsic rewards, such as the enjoyment of hearing preferred music and the feeling response to musical stimuli seem effective in developing long-term pursuit of and interest in musical activity. Extrinsic rewards such as gold stars and first chair assignments in performance organizations prove useful for encouraging and motivating learning. Other rewards do not fit neatly into either of these two classifications. Achieving approval of peers, teachers, and parents is a reward that often accompanies musical performance. Also, the physical exertion and bodily motion of playing an instrument often feel good to the performer. Rewards or positive reinforcement seem likely to be more successful than punishment and threats of punishment in encouraging students to learn (32)(63).

Problems in the use of reward or reinforcement include timing and individual differences. Immediate rewards tend to be more functional than rewards promised in the distant future, especially for some students. A particular object or event may not be rewarding to all students and the same student may not be susceptible to the same reward at different times (69)(32). This means rewards must be chosen carefully and tested for effectiveness while being applied.

Teachers may influence student motivation by choosing appropriate teaching techniques, materials, and attitudes. A recent investigation examined the effect of written practice instructions on time spent practicing and on performance achievement. Playing tests, challenges for chairs in the section, letter grades, and verbal instructions were used to encourage one group to practice. The same devices, plus a written plan for practice were used for the other. The students who had studied with the written practice plan were not found to differ significantly from the other group in amount of practice time or in performance skill (37).

The teacher who wants to use material that may motivate students to persevere in their study of instrumental music can make use of information about tunes that students like. One study examined band method books, analyzing characteristics of tunes that beginning wind instrument students liked most and those they liked least. Best liked were active tunes such as the *Marines Hymn*. The tunes liked best were usually written by well-known composers, had harmony parts, were varied in pitch, dynamics, and rhythm, and contained more variety of form and contrast than the lesser liked tunes. The least liked tunes were nursery rhymes and similar songs (22).

Concepts of Sound: Models

In order to learn how to play a musical instrument, the student must develop a concept of the sound he desires to produce. Auditory models provide the only known method to develop an idea of how a specific instrument should sound. Words cannot describe the sound of a bassoon, a crescendo, a harmonic cadence, or a diminished chord. This leads to a belief that an effective technique for teaching instrumental music is to provide auditory models for students (49). Excellent recording and playback equipment, and the many fine recordings of a wide variety of music now available, provide the teacher with an array of models to use in instruction. Some effects of recorded models are shown in an investigation of two methods of teaching band. One method used drill, repetition, and verbal instructions from the teacher; the other also used these techniques and, in addition, had the students listen to recorded models of the music being learned. Equally difficult musical selections were studied for equal periods of time and then recorded. A panel of experts listened to the recordings. They judged those performances that had been prepared with the aid of recorded models as superior in expression, accuracy, intonation, balance, and general effect to those rehearsed without recorded music (16).

Massed Versus Spaced Practice

What is the optimum length and spacing of practice periods? Research indicates that several relatively short periods of practice are more beneficial than an equal amount of time spent in a few long practice sessions (62)(14).

Further evidence concerning the distribution of practice of learning periods comes from research in the psychobiology of learning. There is a period of time during which short-term memories (mainly newly learned materials or patterns) are fragile. During this time, which is required for consolidation of what is called the memory trace (necessary for long-term remembering), the learning can be reduced by physical trauma and by trying to learn additional material. Data thus far indicate that ". . . the old adage that 'in a lecture few souls are saved after the first fifteen minutes' can be used as a rule of thumb—very few experiences per hour can be consolidated as far as we now know . . . " (56). Instruction, rehearsal, and practice usually will be most effective if divided into relatively short periods of effort spaced over intervals of time. Long, single periods of practice are not efficient ways to develop skills and knowledge.

Effects of Prestudy and Analysis

In part of a series of investigations of memorizing piano music, nine competent young adult pianists were used as subjects. The effects of prestudy of material to be learned and mental rehearsal (imaginary practice) at different times during the learning process were studied (64)(65). Analysis of the material before practice proved of value. Mental rehearsal helped most when done about midway through the practice session. Mental rehearsal after practice to a good performance level seemed of little value. According to these results, a valuable way to practice or rehearse instrumental music may be to start with an examination of the music, followed in turn by practice, mental rehearsal, and further practice. More investigation among secondary and elementary school students is needed to validate these suggestions.

The Beta Hypothesis and Negative Practice

The *Beta* hypothesis suggests that learners might profit from practicing their errors if they pay attention to the fact that they are practicing errors that need to be corrected in future performance. Research in some skills (such as typing) indicates this to be a useful technique, but little research had been done in applying it in music. A single report describes a person who practiced errors in an effort to eradicate them. His attempt was unsuccessful, as the errors persisted in the normal performance situation (73).

Somewhat related to the *Beta* hypothesis is a study of the effects of negative practice on band instruments. Players were asked to practice unfamiliar tunes in several negative ways. One was to play all the tones as eighth notes no matter how they were written; another was to ignore the key signature. In each case the students were to think about their errors and try to imagine how the music would sound if played correctly. Students who practiced negatively made more performance errors than those who practiced in an ordinary manner. The more intelligent the student, the more errors negative practice led him to make (36). Thus research advises the teacher not to encourage negative practice, either in the form of practicing specific errors that occur in attempts at correct performance, or in the form of practicing music in ways different from the notation.

14

Overlearning

Music teachers sometimes suggest students should rehearse tunes repeatedly immediately after learning them. "Play it again to make sure you remember it" is a typical suggestion. A number of studies of the effect of overlearning cast some doubt on the value of this practice. In a series of studies of overlearning in piano performance, students practiced more than was necessary to learn a performance to a criterion level. (One hundred percent overlearning means a tune is repeated, after it has been learned, as many times as it took to learn to play it correctly.) There was no benefit from any of the amounts of overlearning. In later tests those who had practiced only enough to perform correctly did as well as those who had practiced 50, 100, and 200 percent more (65). In a different study seventh and eighth grade cornet and trumpet students overlearned by 50 and 100 percent tunes they had memorized. Neither amount of overlearning was of any value in later performance. In this study students were tested two weeks after and again four weeks after learning the tunes. The performance test at two weeks served as a review for the later performance. The review improved performance on the later test, and was most beneficial for those students judged low in learning ability (7). These findings imply that review is most valuable for the students at the low end of the normal range of ability to learn.

In general, the results of studies of overlearning indicate that there is no value in repeating a tune over and over immediately after it has been learned, although occasional review sessions are of value.

Whole and Part Methods

The relative merits of whole and part methods of learning have been studied in a number of musical situations, with differing results. The whole method has the student play the entire tune each time he practices it. The part method has him divide the tune into short segments, practice each segment as an individual unit, and play the entire tune only after the segments have been learned. Investigation using piano students as subjects indicates that the relative efficiency of the two methods depends in part on the total length of the material to be learned. Short tunes, ranging from eight to about thirty measures in length, seem best learned by the whole method, while longer tunes seem best learned through the part approach (11).

15

In a study of the influence of using whole and part methods to memorize and on subsequent stage fright, short and long tunes were used as learning material. The whole method proved more efficient than the part method in memorizing both short and long tunes, although the advantage was appreciably greater in memorizing the shorter tunes. Neither method was superior in reducing stage fright. An important incidental finding, however, is that the students enjoyed practicing by the whole method more than by the part approach (6).

The whole-part comparisons have the following implications. Students report they enjoy practicing by the whole method more than the part method; thus the whole approach is useful in motivating students to practice specific tunes and to develop positive attitudes toward learning music. For tunes that are not too long, the whole method is usually more efficient than the part method. Compositions that are too long to be practiced as wholes should be broken into as few segments as practical, and these segments practiced as wholes, with each segment related as much as possible to the total composition. More research is needed to confirm and refine understanding of these relationships, and to discover whether they are true for beginners as well as for advanced students.

Drill

Some beginning instrumental instruction is characterized by drill, in which the student is asked to practice a small musical pattern repeatedly. The performance of actual works of music often occurs only after extensive drill. A number of research studies compare the effectiveness of drill with other methods of teaching beginning instrumental students.

One such study compared the drill method with a known-melody method. In the known-melody method, tunes familiar to the students were used in instruction. The students were allowed to select the tunes to be played. The teacher showed the student the correct fingerings or positions for the instrument and the formation of the correct embouchure. After each playing of a melody, an explanation of errors was made to improve the next attempt. After a melody was played at a previously established level of competency, a new tune was introduced. The drill method confined the instruction to formal drill, scales, and exercises such as are found in many instruction books. Melodies were not assigned at any time. At the end of an eighteen-week instructional period, the students taught by the known-melody method were well ahead of those instructed by the drill method. The "known-melody students" successfully covered more than twice as much material, performed more difficult music, developed a more positive attitude toward music, and exhibited substantially larger scores on the *Kwalwasser-Ruch Test of Musical Accomplishment* (59).

Another investigation compared a traditional drill method based on the *Waller String Class Method* with an exploratory, eclectic method for teaching beginners to play violin. The exploratory method used the same book, but de-emphasized drill and repetition and used supplementary finger patterns, position work, bowing variants, and rote songs. After an academic year and a summer of instruction, the students were judged by expert violinists. The eclectic-method students had gained appreciably more than drill-method students in sight-reading, and somewhat more in lefthand and bow arm technique. The groups developed equal skill in tone quality and intonation (8).

These studies concerning drill methods indicate the existence of several other methods that seem to produce better results. Whether the better results are due to the novelty of the methods, differences in the structure of the material, or from motivation arising from playing tunes rather than tones, it seems that the repetitive drill of many instructional methods weakens their effectiveness.

Learning How to Learn

The belief that students can learn how to learn has been validated in several subject fields. An investigation of the effect of special instruction on speed, transfer, and retention in memorizing songs may be applicable to instrumental learning as well. College-level singers were taught how to memorize. Instructions included: (a) approach the music as a whole; (b) analyze form, words, rhythm, dynamics, and melodic contour; (c) give attention to intermediate goals in learning; and (d) self-test early by unaccompanied recitation. Singers following these instructions achieved significantly more in speed of memorization and degree of retention than did a group of singers who had not had the special instruction (76). These results suggest that music teachers might devote more time to teaching students how to learn independently.

17

The teacher who wants to teach his students to think for themselves may find advice in the cognitive development studies made by Piaget and his followers. There seems to be a general pattern in the growth of skill in reasonable thinking. Children between the ages of about two and seven exhibit preoperational thought. The time between the ages of seven and eleven (about grades two through seven) is labeled the period of concrete operations. During this time the child develops skill in logical operations, including classification skills. Classification skills depend partly on an ability called "conservation," which is an awareness that certain properties of objects remain unchanged even though the form of the objects is changed (33)(80).

According to Piaget's studies, the child develops truly logical formal reasoning procedures during the age period of about eleven to fifteen years (55). Although further research is needed to validate more completely this apparent developmental pattern, information to date indicates that teaching methods based on demonstration of logical relationships and explanation of reasons may be relatively unproductive in elementary school instrumental music, somewhat productive in junior high school, but useful for students of senior high school age.

Educational Technology

Programed Instruction

Today's technology provides an increasing variety of instructional media and materials for programed instruction. Research has examined programed textbooks, programed instruction using teaching machines, and various nonprogramed mechanical devices for teaching musical performance. Programed texts and teaching machines have been used in two major ways. First, they supplemented the teacher and regular classroom instruction, and second, they replaced the teacher for certain kinds of instruction.

An extensive study developed a programed text and tested the effectiveness of it in teaching rudiments and basic music theory to college nonmusic majors in piano class. The programed text was applied, tested, and revised several times. Students who studied one semester with the final revision of the programed text achieved as much as a group of students who studied in a traditional class. A third group of students who used the programed material and also had to face instruction achieved

18

more than those who had either classroom or programed instruction (31). These results imply at least two things: (a) a well-constructed programed text can equal the teacher in some instances; and (b) such a text can supplement the teacher, leading to better learning than either the teacher or the text alone stimulates.

Another study compared the achievement of college students who learned fundamentals of music theory from programed materials with the achievement of students who had teacher-classroom instruction. The groups did not differ in amount of learning over a two-week period, but the group using the programed materials took significantly less time to learn (3). Similar results appeared in a study that compared programed and nonprogramed instruction in a college Introduction to Music class (74).

During a course in music fundamentals one academic quarter long, programed materials were used to supplement the instruction in music notation for one week about midway through the term. Students who had the supplemental material scored significantly higher on examinations immediately after using the programed materials and on the course final examination than students who had not used the supplemental material (5).

Research into programed instruction in melodic dictation compared the effectiveness of branching and linear programs. The branching and linear programing techniques were not found to differ in effectiveness, but first-year students who had the programed instruction in ear training achieved more than students who were taught in class (12).

Programed instruction using tape recorded models and instructions for practice was tested in a study of grade school violin students. Tunes of equivalent difficulty were practiced for equal amounts of time, but half were practiced using tape recorded instructions and models, while the other half were practiced normally. After practice sessions spread over several weeks, the tunes were recorded and the recordings judged by a panel of expert violinists. The tunes practiced with the aid of the program were judged significantly better played than the others in phrasing and bowing, tempo, intonation, rhythm, expression, and tone quality (57).

The effect of teaching clarinet fingerings by machine to musically experienced college students who had not had previous clarinet experience has been investigated. One group was taught fingerings in class by a teacher; the second group learned fingering from a teaching machine while using the clarinet without a mouthpiece; and the third learned from the machine but had the clarinet with mouthpiece while learning. All three groups met in class with the teacher to learn about embouchure, and holding and blowing the instrument. All three groups made significant gains in knowledge of fingerings, but no group gained appreciably more than the others (77).

Overt responses on the part of learners is a feature of programed instruction, and research findings tend to confirm its value. In learning woodwind fingerings from a programed text, some students were asked to draw in the fingerings as they were presented, while others were not required to make overt responses. Those who had had no prior woodwind experience learned better when required to fill in the fingerings in the book. There was no significant difference in learning for students who had had woodwind experience (9).

From the research cited, it becomes apparent that teaching machines and programed instruction can be useful in teaching instrumental music. Programs can be used to supplement class-work and increase the learning of a student during a given time. Research shows that aspects of music such as note names and fingerings can be taught effectively by programed books or machines. Judicious use of such programs could enable teachers to devote a greater portion of their time to those parts of the instructional program that require teacher assistance for greatest effect.

Nonprogramed Technical Devices

Various media have proved useful in assisting instrumental instruction. A tachistoscope method and a drill method were used to teach third graders to play flutophone in an eighteen-week series of forty-minute group lessons. Twenty-five minutes of each lesson were identical in both methods; the remainder of the time was devoted to tachistoscope work or drill. Students who worked with the tachistoscope made significantly greater progress in acquiring melodic and rhythmic sight-playing skills (21).

Instrumental students in the intermediate grades were taught clarinet by two methods. One method made use of a variety of audiovisual aids, and the other spent an equal amount of time in conventional instruction. At the end of twelve weeks of instruction students who had been taught by the two methods did not differ significantly in performance, but those who had had the audiovisual instruction made a significant gain in factual knowledge about the clarinet (28). Use of an instructional film was found effective in teaching posture and left-hand position to a group of beginning trumpet students (10). In a study of the use of 8mm film loops to teach identification of clarinet fingering, embouchure, and position errors, students with prior clarinet experience benefitted from the film, while the inexperienced did not (20). The latter result may be interpreted to mean that indiscriminate application of instructional devices to all students is often unsuccessful.

Several studies have examined the use of particular audio and/or visual devices in teaching students to play instruments. One used oscilloscopic transparencies as visual patterns for developing good tone qualities in clarinet players between the ages of nine and fifteen years. The transparencies were made from oscilloscope tracings of a good clarinet tone. Students then performed while observing their own tones on an oscilloscope, trying to match the patterns of their tones with those of the models. This study did not compare the effectiveness of this technique with other ways of teaching tone production, but the investigator asserted his belief that students using this technique developed satisfactory tones in eight weeks, whereas his typical students in that age group usually took two to three years (70). In another study, no differences in intonation were found to result from three different bases of tuning: (a) visual feedback from a Stroboconn; (b) listening for beats with a reference tone played by an electric organ; or (c) a traditional tuning method using student and teacher listening skill (42). Players have difficulty tuning when the tuning note presented is a pure tone; they succeed better when the timbre of the tuning tone is similar to the tone of the instrument being tuned (27).

Results of studies of programed instruction and the use of various instructional devices have at least two important implications for the music teacher: (a) there are some instructional programs and devices that supplement traditional methods of class or private instruction, (b) there are other instructional programs and devices that are equal in effect to traditional classroom or private instruction. Use of these programs and devices can free instructional time for other pursuits in which the teacher is essential. In both cases, the proper use of instructional technology seems to lead to more effective instruction in instrumental music.

Outcomes of Instruction

Teachers are often asked about the values of instrumental music education. Both musical and nonmusical outcomes are sometimes claimed. Most obvious, perhaps, is acquisition of skill in playing a musical instrument. Sometimes listed also are skills in learning to listen and preparation for leisure-time activity in adult life. Results of research provide information about outcomes in several of these areas.

Performance Skills

Although an obvious result of instrumental music education may be development of skill in playing a specific instrument, few attempts have been made to develop specific devices to measure performance skill. One study reports the development of a test for measurement of skill in rhythmic sight-playing (3). The *Watkins-Farnum Performance Scale* represents an attempt to develop a standardized test of performance skill on wind and percussion instruments, and most recently on string instruments as well. The manual for this scale (forms A and B) provides norms for instrumentalists at several grade levels. Little research data exist that suggest how much and in what ways students increase their performance skills through participation in instrumental music at the secondary school level.

Listening Skills

Does performance experience develop listening skills? One study investigated recognition of repeated and altered thematic materials in music by high school and college students who had had different kinds, combinations, and amounts of performance and listening experience. The recognition skills measured were not closely related to performance experience. Many years of experience in performance groups seemed necessary before the appreciable increases in recognition became apparent (23). Another study found that a year of high school instrumental experience had little effect on improving scores on the *Aliferis Music Achievement Test*, a test that asks students to listen and match auditory musical stimuli with printed note patterns (18). When high school instrumentalists were asked to discriminate between differences in the quality of tones coming from three different speakers in high fidelity sound systems, those students with greater amounts of musical experience did not display greater skill in discrimination (44). The results of these studies suggest that listening skill does not necessarily develop in the instrumental music class.

However, other studies show that it is possible to teach instrumental music classes so that a variety of music learnings takes place. Increased perception of aesthetic elements in recorded music has been found to accompany participation in school performance groups (47). An exploratory program in instrumental music increased elementary school students' skills in discriminating instrumental timbre (38). The results of these studies show that skills other than performance on a specific instrument can be taught in an instrumental music class if attention is directed specifically to them.

Preliminary research indicates that teachers can devote some of their rehearsal time to teaching specifically for nonperformance goals without lowering the performance level of their ensembles. Two high school bands of about equal competence (equalized on the basis of intelligence test scores, teacher ratings, and a standardized test of musical ability) were organized. As they prepared for a performance, these bands studied and rehearsed ten works over a thirteen-week instructional period. One of the works was selected for a pre- and posttest, and recorded by each band at the beginning and the end of the thirteen-week period. During the instructional period one band practiced normally for full rehearsal periods. The other devoted ten minutes of each rehearsal period to discussion of the music. Discussion included form, style, ˙interpretation, composers, history, and theory. The pre- and posttest recordings were arranged in random order and judged on rating scales by a panel of instrumental music teachers. Both bands exhibited significant gains in performance rating from pre- to posttest, but they did not differ significantly from each other in the quality of the posttest performance (17).

Dropouts and Carryover

Many students who begin instrumental music instruction drop out of music before high school graduation. Others continue until they graduate, but do not continue to play their instruments in adult life. Investigations of dropouts provide data for particular geographical areas and particular times. The varied results make generalization difficult. One technique has been to ask former students to choose from a list the reasons that caused them to

23

drop out of instrumental music. Teacher and parent opinions about reasons for dropping out also have been solicited. If the students' reports are candid, their opinions should provide a good index of why they dropped out. The studies should be interpreted in light of the fact that the investigators' lists may have failed to include all the reasons that were important to students, parents, or teachers.

In one study, 69 percent of elementary school students who had dropped instrumental music indicated their instruments were difficult to play, and 34 percent said they had dropped out because of this reason. In the music teachers' opinions, 55 percent of the dropout was due to loss of interest, 27 percent due to lack of ability to do the work, 12 percent due to illness, 4 percent due to miscellaneous reasons, and 2 percent due to financial problems (46). Several other studies also found lack of interest to be a major reason for dropping out (78)(58)(13). Other reasons cited included schedule conflicts (39) and lack of time to participate and perform (78).

In one sense, studies of the carryover of instrumental performance into adult life are not encouraging. Many of the students who take part in school instrumental groups do not continue to perform after leaving school. However, similar results are found also in studies of other high school subjects; in that sense the results are not discouraging. One study indicates that although persons who participated in high school music performance activities also tended to participate in musical performance activities as adults, the amount of training while in high school had no important relationship to the amount of time devoted to listening or participation in adult life (51). Another investigation selected two groups from adults who had participated in high school music. One group was composed of those who continued much participation as adults, the other of those whose adult participation was rated as low. The high school music experiences of these two groups proved to be much the same. The most noticeable differences seemed to be (a) persons in the low participation group indicated negative reactions to questions about their emotional and intellectual responses to the music they had performed, and (b) persons in the low participation group indicated that the initial choice of the instrument they played was made by the instructor, with this choice in many cases being unsatisfactory (24). Recent research found that of those questioned who play in adult life, self-taught musicians comprise

24

the highest percentage. The second highest percentage were pianists who played other instruments too, and the third highest percentage were string players (41).

The Need for Further Research

Many needs and opportunities exist for research and development in instrumental music instruction. Replication and extension of the studies on which this report is based would validate and increase confidence in what is "known" about teaching instrumental music. Many areas of instrumental instruction provide opportunities to develop programed book- and machine-based instruction, and media-assisted instructional techniques. Only a few studies have examined development of children's cognitions about music. Little existing research concerns critical periods in music learning, the muscle learning involved in musical performance, or the relationship of physical maturation and instrumental performance. Another field for study concerns attitudes: what are the sources of children's attitudes toward instrumental music, and how does instrumental experience influence children's attitudes toward other facets of music?

Further explorations of developmental patterns of musical perception seem potentially useful. Attempts to predict success in performance might be expanded to include a greater proportion of measures from the affective and psychomotor areas. Understanding of the dropout and carryover problems might be enhanced by investigation of reasons for continuing, rather than of reasons for discontinuing. Development of more accurate and discriminating measures of musical performance promises many benefits for instruction and research. And, perhaps, valuable knowledge would accrue from research that tests some of the basic assumptions of instrumental music education. Is it true that "of a certainty, performance of music must be the essence of instruction in music . . ." (15)? What uniquenesses has instrumental instruction to offer in music education?

Beyond the need for extensive research lies a need for development. Research results, to influence instruction, must be packaged, field-tested, and distributed in usable form. Reports such as *From Research to the Music Classroom* are one sort of packaging and distribution. The development and dissemination of programed instructional sequences, media-associated lessons,

25

test batteries for measurement and diagnosis, and particular instructional techniques seem especially important. Music education traditionally has not enjoyed the position of industries, which devote substantial effort to research and development. Rather, music education research typically has been done as part of some individual's academic study toward an advanced degree. As a result, series of studies focused on specific areas of knowledge are rare. The development of research focus, sustained investigation, and development and dissemination of packages based on the results have great promise for improving instrumental music education.

References

1. Allen, Eleanor B., *A Study of the Perception of Instrumental Tone Color by Children of Nursery School Age.* Master's Thesis, University of Kansas, 1959.
2. Anastasiow, N.J. and R.F. Shambaugh, "Experimental Use of Pre-Instrumental Music Melody Instruments," *Journal of Research in Music Education,* Vol. 13 (Winter 1965), pp. 246-248.
3. Ashford, T.H.A., "The Use of Programed Instruction to Teach Fundamental Concepts in Music Theory," *Journal of Research in Music Education,* Vol. 14 (Fall 1966), pp. 171-177.
4. Ausherman, Robert D., *A Study of the Ability of Secondary School Students to Perceive Differences in Tone Quality of the Same Instrument.* Master's Thesis, University of Kansas, 1956.
5. Barnes, Robert A., "Programed Instruction in Music Fundamentals for Future Elementary Teachers," *Journal of Research in Music Education,* Vol. 12 (Fall 1964), pp. 187-198.
6. Beck, William, *Whole and Part Methods of Memorizing Music in Relation to Stage Fright.* Master's Thesis, University of Kansas, 1945.
7. Becker, W.R., *The Effect of Overlearning, Initial Learning Ability and Review upon the Musical Memory of Junior High School Cornet and Trumpet Players.* Doctoral Dissertation, State University of Iowa, 1962.
8. Beene, Don W., *A Comparison of Two Models of Teaching*

26

Beginning Violin Classes. Master's Thesis, University of Kansas, 1964.

9. Bigham, William M. Jr., *A Comparison of Two Response Modes in Learning Woodwind Fingerings by Programmed Text.* Doctoral Dissertation, Florida State University, 1965.

10. Boley, D.M., *The Development and Evaluation of the Effectiveness of a Pilot Instructional Sound-Film for Teaching Beginning Trumpet Students with a Brief Survey of the History of Trumpet Instruction and the History of Educational Film Research.* Doctoral Dissertation, University of Iowa, 1970.

11. Brown, R.W., "A Comparative Study of 'Whole' and 'Part,' and 'Combination,' Methods of Learning Piano Music," *Journal of Experimental Psychology,* Vol. II (1928), pp. 235-247.

12. Carlsen, James, "Programed Learning in Melodic Dictation," *Journal of Research in Music Education,* Vol. 12 (Summer 1964), pp. 139-148.

13. Casey, George J. Jr., *A Study of Instrumental Music Drop-outs of the Moline (Illinois) Public Schools.* Doctoral Dissertation, Colorado State College, 1964.

14. Childs, C.A., *A Comparison of Two Distributed Instructional Periods in the Teaching of Beginning Instrumental Music Students.* Doctoral Dissertation, Colorado State College, 1963.

15. Choate, Robert A., Research in Music Education. *Journal of Research in Music Education,* Vol. 13 (Summer 1965), pp. 67-86.

16. Clinesmith, Carl B., *Phonograph Records as Aids in the Musical Development of a High School Band.* Master's Thesis, University of Kansas, 1950.

17. Coleman, E.L., *Some Effects of Teaching Musical Knowledge in a Performance Class.* Master's Thesis, University of Kansas, 1966.

18. Colwell, Richard, "An Investigation of Musical Achievement Among Vocal Students, Vocal-Instrumental Students, and Instrumental Students," *Journal of Research in Music Education,* Vol II (Fall 1963), pp. 123-130.

19. Cramer, William F., *The Relation of Maturation and Other Factors to Achievement in Beginning Instrumental Music Performance at the Fourth Through Eighth Grade Levels.* Doctoral Dissertation, Florida State University, 1958.

20. Diamond, Robert M. and Thomas C. Collins, "The Use of 8mm Loop Films to Teach the Identification of Clarinet Fingering, Embouchure, and Hand Position Errors," *Journal of Research in Music Education,* Vol. 15 (Fall 1967), pp. 224-228.

21. DiFronzo, Robert F., *A Comparison of Tachistoscopic and Conventional Methods in Teaching Grade Three Music Sight-Playing on a Melody Wind Instrument.* Doctoral Dissertation, University of Connecticut, 1966.

22. Downing, Bobby M., *The Tune Choices of Beginning Wind Instrumental Music Students.* Doctoral Dissertation, Colorado State College, 1965.

23. Duerksen, George L., "Recognition of Repeated and Altered Thematic Materials in Music," *Journal of Research in Music Education,* Vol. 16 (Spring 1968), pp. 3-30.

24. Falkner, K.W., *The Influence of Music Education and Private Study on Adult Interest in Music in Two Selected Communities.* Doctoral Dissertation, State University of Iowa, 1957.

25. Froseth, James O., *An Investigation of the Use of Musical Aptitude Profile Scores in the Instruction of Beginning Students in Instrumental Music.* Doctoral Dissertation, University of Iowa, 1968.

26. George, Warren E., *Significant Predictors for College Achievement in Specified Areas of Music Education and Identification of Potential Graduates.* Doctoral Dissertation, University of Kansas, 1969.

27. Greer, R.D., *The Effect of Timbre on Brass-Wind Intonation.* Doctoral Dissertation, University of Michigan, 1969.

28. Grimm, Guss L., *An Experiment in Teaching the Clarinet with Audio-visual Aids.* Master's Thesis, University of Kansas, 1949.

29. Groff, Frank, *Effect on Academic Achievement of Excusing Elementary School Pupils from Class to Study Instrumental Music.* Doctoral Dissertation, University of Connecticut, 1963.

30. Gutsch, Kenneth U., "Evaluation in Instrumental Performance: An Individual Approach," *Bulletin of the Council for Research in Music Education,* No. 4 (1965).

31. Hargiss, Genevieve F., "The Acquisition of Sight Singing Ability in Piano Classes for Students Preparing to be Elementary Teachers," *Journal of Research in Music Educa-*

tion, Vol. 10 (Spring 1962), pp. 69-75.

32. Hilgard, E.R. and G.H. Bower, *Theories of Learning.* New York: Appleton Century Crofts, 1966, p. 563.

33. Hoffman, Martin L. and Lois W. Hoffman, *Review of Child Development Research.* New York: Russell Sage Foundation, 1964.

34. Hutcherson, Rita J., *Group Instruction in Piano: An Investigation of the Relative Effectiveness of Group and Individual Piano Instruction at the Beginning Level.* Doctoral Dissertation, State University of Iowa, 1955.

35. Jacobs, Camille, "Investigation of Kinesthetics in Violin Playing," *Journal of Research in Music Education,* Vol. 17 (Spring 1969), pp. 112-114.

36. Johnson, Gordon B., "Negative Practice on Band Instruments: An Exploratory Study," *Journal of Research in Music Education,* Vol. 10 (Fall 1962), pp. 100-104.

37. Johnson, Robert E., *A Comparison of Two Methods of Motivating Instrumental Music Students to Practice.* Master's Thesis, University of Kansas, 1965.

38. Kersey, Robert E., "Effects of an Exploratory Program in Instrumental Music on the Aural Perception of Instrumental Timbre," *Journal of Research in Music Education,* Vol. 14 (Winter 1966), pp. 303-308.

39. Kruth, Edwin C., *Student Drop-out in Instrumental Music in the Secondary Schools of Oakland, California.* Doctoral Dissertation, Stanford University, 1964.

40. Lamp, Charles J., *The Determination of Aptitude for Specific Musical Instruments.* Doctoral Dissertation, University of California, Berkeley, 1933.

41. Lawrence, Sidney J. and Nadia Dachinger, "Factors Relating to Carryover of Musical Training into Adult Life," *Journal of Research in Music Education,* Vol. 15 (Spring 1967), pp. 23-31.

42. Lester, William Jr., *A Comparison of Three Methods for Improving Intonation in the Performance of Instrumental Music.* Doctoral Dissertation, University of Colorado, 1963.

43. Luce, John R., "Sight-Reading and Ear-Playing Abilities as Related to Instrumental Music Students," *Journal of Research in Music Education,* Vol. 13 (Summer 1965), pp. 101-109.

44. Lutte, Larry E., *The Ability of High School Instrumental Students to Discriminate Differences in Tone Quality of*

Three Different Phonograph Speaker Systems. Master's Thesis, University of Kansas, 1967.

45. Manor, H.C., "A Study in Prognosis: The Guidance Value of Selected Measures of Musical Aptitude, Intelligence, Persistence, and Achievement in Tonette and Adaption Classes for Prospective Instrumental Students," *Journal of Educational Psychology*, Vol. 41 (1950), pp. 31-50.

46. Martignetti, Anthony J., "Causes of Elementary Instrumental Music Dropouts," *Journal of Research in Music Education*, Vol. 13 (Fall 1965), pp. 117-183.

47. McCarthy, K.J., *Effect of Participation in School Music Performance Organizations on the Ability to Perceive Aesthetic Elements in Recorded Music.* Doctoral Dissertation, Case Western Reserve University, 1969.

48. McCoy, W.L., *A Comparison of Select Psychomotor Abilities of a Sample of Undergraduate Music Majors and a Sample of Undergraduate Nonmusic Majors.* Doctoral Dissertation, Louisiana State University, 1970.

49. Merriam, Alan P., *The Anthropology of Music.* Evanston: Northwestern University Press, 1964, pp. 145-163.

50. Mitchum, John, *The Wing 'Standardised Tests of Musical Intelligence'; An Investigation of Predictability with Selected Seventh Grade Beginning Band Students.* Doctoral Dissertation, Florida State University, 1969.

51. Neal, Charles D., *Carryover of Musical Activities Following Graduation from High School.* Doctoral Dissertation, Indiana University, 1948.

52. Pence, Don P., *A Study to Determine the Optimum Grade for Beginning Class Study of Wind Instruments.* Master's Thesis, University of Kansas, 1942.

53. Petzold, Robert G., "The Development of Auditory Perception of Musical Sounds by Children in the First Six Grades," *Journal of Research in Music Education*, Vol. II (Spring 1963), pp. 21-43.

54. Petzold, Robert G., "The Perception of Music Symbols in Music Reading by Normal Children and by Children Gifted Musically," *Journal of Experimental Education*, Vol. 28, No. 4 (1960), pp. 271-319.

55. Piaget, Jean, *Psychology of Intelligence.* Paterson: Littlefield, Adams & Company, 1963, p. 123.

56. Pribram, Karl H., "Neurological Notes on the Art of Educating," *Theories of Learning and Instruction*, E.R.

Hilgard, ed., Chicago: University of Chicago Press, 1964, pp. 78-110.

57. Purmort, Barbara A., *The Development and Use of Programed Violin Instruction.* Master's Thesis, University of Kansas, 1967.

58. Reckart, Garland, B. Jr., *A Study of Instrumental Music Dropouts.* Master's Thesis, University of Kansas, 1965.

59. Reimer, Alvin J., *A Comparison of Two Methods of Teaching Instrumental Music to Beginners.* Master's Thesis, University of Kansas, 1944.

60. Rhoades, Fordyce L., *An Evaluation of Measures for the Prediction of Success in Instrumental Music Study.* Master's Thesis, University of Washington, 1938.

61. Roper, Bueford T., *A Comparative Analysis of the Attitudes and Musical Progress of Two Instrumental Groups.* Master's Thesis, University of Kansas, 1950.

62. Rubin-Rabson, Grace, "Studies in the Psychology of Memorizing Piano Music, II: A Comparison of Massed and Distributed Practice," *Journal of Educational Psychology,* Vol. 31 (1940), pp. 270-284.

63. Rubin-Rabson, Grace, "Studies in the Psychology of Memorizing Piano Music IV: The Effects of Incentive," *Journal of Educational Psychology,* Vol. 32 (1941), pp. 45-54.

64. Rubin-Rabson, Grace, "Studies in the Psychology of Memorizing Piano Music V: A Comparison of Pre-Study Periods of Varied Length," *Journal of Educational Psychology,* Vol. 32 (1941), pp. 101-112.

65. Rubin-Rabson, Grace, "Studies in the Psychology of Memorizing Piano Music VI: A Comparison of Two Forms of Mental Rehearsal and Keyboard Overlearning," *Journal of Educational Psychology,* Vol 32 (1941), pp. 593-602.

66. Sell, Marion W., *Preference for Band and Orchestra as an Esthetic Medium for Music Among Public School Students.* Master's Thesis, University of Kansas, 1950.

67. Shugert, James M., *An Experimental Investigation of Heterogeneous Class and Private Methods of Instruction with Beginning Instrumental Music Students.* Doctoral Dissertation, University of Illinois, 1969.

68. Sims, Francis J., *An Experimental Investigation of the Relative Effectiveness of Group and Individual Voice Instruction at the Beginning Level to High School Students.* Doctoral Dissertation, University of Oklahoma, 1961.

31

69. Skinner, B.F., *The Technology of Teaching.* New York: Appleton Century Crofts, 1968, pp. 145-168.

70. Small, Terence S., "The Evaluation of Clarinet Tone Through the Use of Oscilloscopic Transparencies," *Journal of Research in Music Education,* Vol. 15 (Spring 1967), pp. 11-22.

71. Tietze, William B., *The Effect of Pre-Band Melody and Rhythm Instruments on the Musical Learning of Beginning Fourth Grade Instrumental Students.* Doctoral Dissertation, State University of Iowa, 1958.

72. Waa, Loren Roger, *An Experimental Study of Class and Private Methods of Instruction In Instrumental Music.* Doctoral Dissertation, University of Illinois, 1965.

73. Wakeham, G., "Query on 'A Revision of the Fundamental Law of Habit Formation," *Science,* Vol. 68. (1928), pp. 135-136.

74. Wardian, J.F., *An Experiment Concerning the Effectiveness of Programmed Learning for Use in Teaching the Fundamentals of Music.* Doctoral Dissertation, Washington State University, 1963.

75. Webster, James B., *A Study of Children's Reasons for Choice of Instrument.* Master's Thesis, University of Kansas, 1954.

76. Williamson, S. Charles, *The Effect of Special Instruction on Speed, Transfer, and Retention in Memorizing Songs.* Doctoral Dissertation, University of Kansas, 1964.

77. Woelflin, Leslie E., "Teaching Clarinet Fingerings with Teaching Machines," *Journal of Research in Music Education,* Vol. 12 (Winter 1964), pp. 287-294.

78. Wolfle, Ernest E. Jr., *Relationships Between Selected Factors and Participation and Non-Participation in Instrumental Music in the Cincinnati Public Schools.* Doctoral Dissertation, Indiana University, 1969.

79. Young, William T., *An Investigation of the Relative and Combined Power of Musical Aptitude, General Intelligence, and Academic Achievement Tests to Predict Musical Attainment.* Doctoral Dissertation, University of Iowa, 1969.

80. Zimmerman, Marilyn Pflederer and Lee Sechrest, "Brief Focused Instruction and Musical Concepts," *Journal of Research in Music Education,* Vol. 18 (Spring 1970), pp. 25-35; Pflederer, Marilyn, "The Responses of Children to Musical Tasks Embodying Piaget's Principle of Conservation," *Journal of Research in Music Education,* Vol. 12 (Winter 1964), pp. 251-268.

UNIVERSITY OF ILLINOIS
LIBRARY